IF LANGUAGE

ISBN 978-0-9737181-6-4

IF LANGUAGE

GREGORY BETTS

FORWARD BY JC BELLRINGER

BookThug
Toronto

Dedicated to the Memory of Gordon E.H. Betts
for whom care was an ethical imperative.

Uncertainty is at the very heart of Gregory Betts'
If Language. In one sense, Betts is the author of these
56 poems, writing them in the traditional sense of
the word, crafting something unique and original
into existence. But in another equally accurate
sense, Betts is not responsible for a single word in
this book, having instead re-arranged every letter
of a paragraph written by the poet Steve McCaffery
into a new order to suit Betts' poetic ambitions. It's
uncertain who wrote these poems, to whom they
belong, which is the most true, or the most deceptive.
This is a text, it seems, where nothing can be trusted.
In so doing, *If Language* asks the type of serpentine
linguistic questions only a poet would ever consider it
necessary – and essential – to answer. What if language
were shuffled and re-shuffled as casually as a deck of
cards? Does language mean all of the things that it
could mean, in all the ways it could be arranged and
re-arranged, both intended and unintended? What if
someone took a passage of writing – about something,
or anything – and forced each letter of each word into
another word in another sentence until, through the
alchemy of the anagram, the entire original passage
about something, or anything, was replaced by a
new passage about a different something, a different
anything? The two passages would be made up of
entirely the same component parts, but whose voice
would be speaking through them? Would the original
meaning be lost or enhanced? And what if someone
did this not once or twice, but 56 times? What if?

The 56 poems of *If Language* seem uncertain
of what, exactly, they want to say and who, exactly,
is speaking. And that is precisely the point. These

poems – as disparate and seemingly unconnected as they may be – share more in common than perhaps any collection of poems in existence. They share an entire set of 525 letters, a poetic bloodline as familial and unbreakable as genetic code. Linked only by this constant constraint, these poems are at once firm and flexible, pulling the reader into sturdy narratives and strange spectacles of language that are both random and inevitable, as words and letters live and die and are reincarnated with each turn of the page.

An extended anagram project of this kind is unique and not without both implicit and explicit limitations, requiring often maddeningly technical determination on behalf of the author. All 525 letters must appear only once in each anagram, and each of them must appear. The letter "i" appears 56 times in each anagram, the most of any individual letter. This type of determined restriction is what gives *If Language* its most subversive layer of meaning, exposing the nearly limitless undercurrent of suggestion that is buried in every utterance, every passage of text. In parsing the form of a single paragraph, Betts has found dozens of alternate realities, each as valid as any other. The resulting 56 anagrams, 56 differing versions of the same thing, are surprisingly resilient to the extreme pressure that is being put upon each and every letter that comprises them; like so much fiction and poetry that is free of such strict constraints, *If Language* demands on unfolding itself into a surprisingly recognizable narrative, resisting and insisting on telling its own story.

Betts relentlessly, enthusiastically shapes and reshapes his vowels and consonants with the temerarious glee of an anarchist, building words and transplanting them into sentences just long enough to tear them apart and start over again. Poets have long been attracted to stringent and complicated forms: the sonnet, the haiku, and even the couplet are all linguistic constraints that have appealed to writers interested in the pressure that can be exerted on and withstood by language, and the arduous and Byzantine beauty that such linguistic acrobatics can create. In *If Language* Betts picks up the cause of the anagram, that elaborate parlour trick, that punk cousin of the lipogram, and elevates a simple device into something magical, forcing meaning and form into it by subjecting it to the punishing conditions of constraint-based poetry.

If Language exposes the possibility of speaking through another's words, or, more precisely, speaking through someone else's letters, through the unintended meaning that inevitably exists inside even the most common and banal of expressions. In this way, *If Language* is not only a unique way of telling but a unique way of listening, as delicate as it is obsessive. Betts disassembles each word gently, with a sensitive and tender ear, listening to the sound of a single paragraph, to the space in it that is both occupied and unoccupied, for omissions and possibilities, for the literal and the poetic, for meanings that are still trapped behind something obvious in a passing phrase or casual remark.

Exactly what Betts finds in those spaces is elusive and not always certain, like the heart of poetry itself. While authorship and voice, even meaning and form itself, are uncertain in *If Language*, the balance struck between McCaffery's parental paragraph and these 56 discrete but intimately connected children is entirely original, and entirely essential.

JC BELLRINGER

The following epigraph by Steve McCaffery contains exactly 525 letters. The page following the quote contains a re-organization of its literal – letteral – constituents, also 525 letters long. The following 56 poems are all perfect anagrams (not including punctuation or capitalisation) of the original quote, which was the theoretical springboard, the palette, the keyboard for this hopeful obsession. The number of poems was determined by the 56 'i's, strangely, appropriately, and uncannily the most frequent letter (there is a complete break-down by letter on the very last page of this manuscript).

'If Language Writing successfully detaches Language from the historical purpose of summarizing global meaning replacing the goal of totality with the free polydynamic drive of parts, it nevertheless falls short in addressing the full implications of this break and seems especially to fail in taking full account of the impact of the human subject with the thresholds of linguistic meaning. It is at the critical locus of productive desire that this writing opens itself up to an alternative 'libidinal' economy which operates across the precarious boundaries of the symbolic and the biological and has its basis in intensities.'

[Steve McCaffery, "Language Writing: from Productive to Libidinal Economy." presented as part of The Festival of Canadian Poetry, State University of New York (Buffalo), October, 1980.]

'aaaaaaaaaaaaaaaaaaaaaaaaaaaaaaaaaaaaaaaaaaaab
bbbbbbbcccccccccccccccccccccdddddddddddddeeeee
eeeeeeeeeeeeeeeeeeeeeeeeeeeeeeeeeeeeeeeeeeeffffffffffffffffffff
gggggggggggggggghhhhhhhhhhhhhhhhhhhhhhhhhhhiiii
iiiiiiiiiiiiiiiiiiiiiiiiiiiiiiiiiiiiiiiiiiiiiiiiijkkllllllllllllllll
llllllllllllllmmmmmmmmmmmmmnnnnnnnnnnnnnnn
nnnnnnnnnnnnnnnnnnoooooooooooooooooooooooooo
oooooooopppppppppppppprrrrrrrrrrrrrrrrrrrrrrrrssssssssss
sssssssssssssssssssssssssssssssssstttttttttttttttttttttttttttttttttttttttttt
tttttttuuuuuuuuuuuuuuuuuuuvvvvwwwwwyyyyyyyz'

CHAPTER ONE

1.

Echo responds trapped in the limits of the **words**
Narcissus sacrifices flippantly. He discounts this
recall of his locution, not hearing a tight **voice**
ripple and tremble, tremble all timid, full of taint,
speak through his big mullock.

'Noise in rotting bush: 'tis someone giggling close.
Who are you?'
'No one.'
'Will you shun me?'
'You shun me!'

'Come hither,' he commands, and she, a petit
infant, bolts in joyful spirits.
'Me,' she says, giggling a pliant craft.

'Desist! I would rather depart this life than abduct
you!'
'Life!'

'Never!' he cries.
'Ever,' Echo pleas, recognizing that Fate will devise
a glacial, fanatic tale to suit. A tacit artist can sift a
basic alibi of a stiff fact.

2.

The futile clown Costard giggles, full of pulse,
to Don Adriano and master Holofernes:

> "O, they have lived long on the alms-basket of words.
> I marvel thy master hath not eaten thee for **a** word;
> for thou art not so long [in] the head as
> honorificabilitudinitatibus."

> *Honorificabilitudinitatibus*

There is an anagram
in his strangely spelt chide:

> *Hi ludi, F. Baconis nati, tuiti orbi*

In English, it claims:

> *These plays keep F. Bacon's offspring for all*

I validate authorship with mutating,
shifting *Rosicrucian* – **secret message** – mechanics.

> Occultist facts multiply,
> elegize Egyptian spells, supply
> Celtic cultism.

> I jostle page effects,
> whisper magic science.

> *[William Shakespeare's <u>Love's Labours Lost</u>, from
> Act Five, Scene One. Anagram noted in Sir Edwin
> Durning-Lawrence's <u>Bacon is Shakespeare</u> (1910)]*

THE SONNETS

Within this factual system I hold this
Curse: I hail portent **limits** aloft.
Verse is a granitic, endemic loss,
Thief of a lying voice; a ghostly cough.

Include in the arsenal the fact of clay.
Disrupt, ban the thermal poet writing.
His cry is a projective fable, body
In titian bath with stale smog, with telling.

Feuds of critic leakage to dodge gaping
Gloom, I echo after iambic chaos.
Alter to combine optic sonnet meaning.
Utilize proprioceptive surplus.

What of man's basic genius goal?
Fault ritual usage, his fusion of soul.

First syllable, first column fulfills the Petrarchan; second, in the middle, is Shakespearean; and third Spenserian.

4.

The economic dream for all linguists is to calculate the sum value of spelling. The charge could, **ironically,** inhibit brain disruption or denotation, dispiriting inspired authors – costing the cult of print a hang-up.

Despite a plea for flat meaning, the body includes itself within the telling, from beneath the work.

Some writing aims to utilize this neglectful imprint as a public acclaim for the sign. Sound poets, the Breath Line, and projective verse all echo that within the assembly of voice is body: flesh. A successful case massages all facts as clay: a goal of chaos.

'If Poetry' uses writing's misreading to fight historian safety, ink faith.

CHAPTER TWO

5.

Reading McCaffery in German. The book is closed, but the poems resonate, echo as internal philosophies, an argument of insidious apparitions. Each one points to Toronto, attach within a transplanted cultural muse-machine.

Day by day, I teach Atwood, cite McCaffery, and re-read Wittgenstein. Still have my visit to Merz-house and the Sistine, to scoff Niagara ice wine on the Rhine, visit blissful Black Forest amblers to figure **where** here is, that here ought to be cliff-tops fulfilling uphill **illusion**. I **toil** in affiliate groups as students compass, grip judgment. All clutch a still cellphone bag; civic digits. I sit high as cliffs light glassily.

6.

I tell my students that the first person to use a word or idea, or publish it, often gets credit for its invention. They earnestly consume this notion, jot everything. Only ask for the origin: to allocate; authorize.

Scanning the room, I tell them whoever **inscribed** it first.

The students are not satisfied, this bluff violates a complicated education formula.

A self-conscious pause, if slightly awkward, highlights a big gap.

I drift.

I begin, chaff, note it's an international principle.

Happier smiles blossom. It is a magical, childish charm. Able pencils flow in successful delight. Each is a human chaos. Pages finally fill up, accumulate epic baggage.

7.

So many times I teach, bagpipe, instead of learn. It's this unwilled forgetfulness, forgetting to hear the cadence of millions build up, branch, crashing against each other; gigantic germs **of** living water swirl.

That time at the lake, the machine. We still haven't insisted upon or considered the insurgence of inscription, if it is even a possibility. Bullshit talk drops air. April's carcass, flees off. Unglamorous organisms chasing the shadow gem. The clouds filled by the pathetic fallacy cover the instinctual onslaught. A pond injustice, a maze of instability. I apocopate our affected **beauty**. Your misfit cool multiplies this foolish thrill.

8.

A Hamilton Spectator editorial on Miki's <u>Surrender</u>
calls it academic, aloof, and false. His writing built,
glows, speculative paradigms and theories too
keen for the scribe **to catch** the vigilant study of
identification to suit her humanistic calling. Accept
in mind that poems *ought* to focus, *grill,* the bard's
self; be a psychoanalytic inspiration of an oppressed
spirit. His duty is to legislate sincerity, invent a self,
and sell it. How it falls short when it conjures the
new! Leave that for science, poets; your gig is a gag.

The final curtain is falling.

Embrace the chill, final maze of Estragon.

Publish huge mouthy bibles of shuffling euphemism.

9.

A manual to interdisciplinary poetry for institutional funding associations.

Poetry: philosophy filtered through private minds and lives, entertainment for the pitiful obsessive, anything that can't classify itself, hates you for asking, a darkling thrush, nationalism veiled in art subsidies, proud of fog, attainable enigma, unread ignored inspired, thought without influence, possible wor(l)ds, elitist half manic craft, aconite gaze, beautiful smelling lies.

The eligible poems for high-school, glib accessible choices, of course, can't touch, whip **magical facts**. Select pages of jewels thrill, cheat schemata, mimic the hottest scrawl.

CHAPTER THREE

10.

For McCaffery, 'Metaphor, in fact, attacks the notion of absolute meaning. At least one aspect of the metaphoric operation involves the institution of an identity between dissimilar things....'

still,

'Paragrams (including anagrams) are .... *figures of antisemantics;* [it is] that aspect of language [that] *escapes* all discourse **and** .... commits [it] unavoidably **to** a general economy.... words within words contests the notion of writing as a creativity, proposing.... a superfluity of signifiers'

The deluded public publish McCaffery's hellish blitz: I flush, grill the jilted debauch; I chisel his tough hull.

I'll **pluck** his fire's **echo**.
I'll change his theories legible

["Writing as a General Economy" 205, and 208-9]

II.

LANGUAGE writing disturbs, jeers, all language
that privileges meaning as **a** necessary destination.
Militant in nature, this body of literature split off
from known codes by disrupting semantic allocation.
This retelling accepts the suppressed implications of
the machine. It fights the sacred theory, challenges
the foolish bubble of value. Lyotard: 'the artistic
vanguard knows that it has no readers, no viewers,
and no listeners.' As communicability afflicts,
communication silences artifice's heliographic flight.

Populist   poets   utilize   soft   euphoria.
LANGUAGE   poems   hail   humility,   filch
off   filth,   flood   hectic   bodies   with   chaos.

*[Jean-François Lyotard and Jean-Loup Thébaud. Just
Gaming. Translated by Wlad Godzich. Theory and
History of Literature Vol. 20. Minneapolis: University
of Minnesota Press, 1980.]*

12.

Hi Steve,

I've been working on your LANGUAGE poetry article of late, applying specific attention to the disparities between the economies of body, libido, and surfaces (language poets' terms). A thick patch of stuff. I wonder, though, isn't it enough to stage a small metaphor for the libidinal process as LANGUAGE in a physical medium? Doesn't it stall such criticism in **voicing** the Other of language rather than the individual, the subject? Its small, chromatic script **flirts**, slips off; clarifies a restful craft's fall. Isn't this **also** how the *libidinal* economy functions within, fills us, and thus the azoic poem has libidinal realism?

Sincerely,

Greg

13.

Realism subjects itself to the regulatory paradigms, ideologies of its implicit world. The Unreal work constructs its own hypothetical principles to govern the internal organization of its configuration. Realism health is assessed by its relationship/ affinity to the beliefs of its conceptual culture. The difference in Unreal health is phrased through its **skilful** consistency and obedience to its own valiant postulate. If it highlights cheapish fun, half-magical anti-Symbolist ideals can claim civil, arid images muffle contempt: have harmful, flawed baggage.

Accurate encoding is but a possible hypothesis and nothing more.

14.

Language breaks narrative trajectory, implodes and spills itself. Where does this occur: in beliefs? the mind? Words surface from the brain that forms its paratactic computation, caps potent allusions. Heidegger argues (and Olson consents) that we dwell in the house of language. If language falters, **as** inevitable, is it thus the mind or, in his metaphor, the condition of being in language that ignites the sylphic instability? The occultic brain is self-sufficient. The muffled allegory flips political customs into civilized mimesis. Instability is thus **a** property of language– cf. a **devilish** itch to hyphen catholic – is mark of a hollow core.

15.

Dear Greg,

A 'libidinal realism' is impossible for libido is the covenant of irreality and parareality. Moreover, the '=' signs amidst the characters spelling LANGUAGE push language past beliefs and into applied **mathematics** and logic. Unit consonance isn't my *Beatrice*. As substitute, I choose how fissure and the doubling of surfeit utilize loss. The swift payoff of economic parlance converts the thrill of plots into philosophic fluff. Does all this simplify things? The language-Other is *objet*, is distinctly Language (which is another caustic inhuman fact) which must link writing to death like a triste erotic to the null.

– Steve McCaffery

CHAPTER FOUR

16.

Today it will be sacrificial; slightly dissented pedantics rushing up from the pre-Cambrian fossilization process will collide with **effervescent** cryogenics to burst into a castrato sky: the inviting wind of immobility. For the afternoon, the golden north may suffer a slight shimmer of late-Fascist nostalgia judging a magnetic attraction for the faithful eunuch of creativity. A mulish land, hope igniting up papacies. Celestial globes highlight a blasphemous annular eclipse illusion. The sun had also a holier ellipsis. Boaters take heed: modification of the collapsing universe threatens to upset the bawdiest circumstances.

17.

Today it will be apostolatic; the office will be closed from noon until the apotheosis. A fifth large build-up of sanguine interstitials will initiate chaos in the consistent chitchat, occluded by the rare conjugation of ghost bulls **and** scorpion cuts in emphatically violet light streams. Campers; be sure to pack your diaglossic emissaries today in preparation for the unveiling precipitations. Which **geometrical** figures offer given thoughts, share in the vibrating spaces. Fresh ill-effects frighten hapless humans. The balls await fulfillment in the imagination and may densify as dusk gets closer and clouds materialize might.

18.

Today it will be music degrees of collage with a litter of sun petroleum and solace, hi-fi of sickishness, obliged by a conservative force that, it is hopeful, will fulminate in the social realities of committed principalities. Someone's parents slip back into an ungracious war front that agitates the alliance and physiognomy of illuminating gases threatening shift. By **tonight,** at the mausoleum parade, the light scoffing carbuncular air should eroticize its partly visible superobjectivism. Plush gallows hiss. There is a fifty percent chance of fifth and eighth dimensions contrasting that should clear up all things considered.

CHAPTER FIVE

19.

Let's reconsider and test a basic linguistic principle. Language is a theory, an attempt to represent all aspects of life in something other than life. It is used to mutually describe and facilitate living. When it is off, as happens for all kinds of reasons, its capricious structuralism emerges. Ideas build upon distortion, pounce such chaos.

Too much time, however, has been given to prove this fallibility, highlight risks that determine the chance of thought.

The theoretical principle of language recognizes how all words fulfill this catalyst job of facilitating life **by** always shifting. Anagrams embody this nomadic functionalism.

CHAPTER SIX

20.

THE SCRABBLELOLOGY

Alfred Mosher Butts (formulas herd Betts) anagrammatician and architect from Poughkeepsie, United States, fashioned a game he called CRISS CROSS WORDS. His playful cryptographic investigation of our language and his original tile distribution system compelled **generations**, billions of

games played. Inventors cherish the profitable titan, its intuitive straightforwardness. Poets energize, launch the waffling effect into lingual callisthenics of cut voices. Students listen to pacific hip-hop, flick oily joints, play in school as legitimate fun.

The unambitious watch with faith, inhale the social milieu.

21.

After Galileo fit his 'perspicillia' telescope,
he saw chaotic facts previously past all seeing sight.

With chilled, cliché Christian officials,
he could not flash any heliocentric suggestions of his find.

Jotting off occultist signs of **this** to Kepler in Tübingen,
G. hid the affair in this palaeographic anagram:
SMAISMRMILME **POET** ALEUMIBUNENUGT TAURIAS
To say: I have discovered that Saturn has two cyclic, lunar bodies

But Kepler disorganized its illicit boffo folio to say:

Savle umbistineum geminatum martia proles

Hello. Burning twins: descendents of the red planet
Or: The red planet has two moons.

By uncanny fate, the latter is right.

22.

Anagrams happen within the symbolic constituents of the word, replacing linear progress for consciousness of being object. Without narrative, the precipitate icon goes to its liminal field between living language and closed thought. It provokes the disguise of the futile stability which **shapes all** of human thought. It discards all **sense** only to utilize fallibility, illustrating the accidental shape of all reality. But my poem's diacritical system re-inscribes punctuation's officious scheme to make official meaning in arched language. Despite anagram's riot locus, plot shifts faith. Hard differences vanish from this thrall.

23.

The Anagram is:

Christian, it re-enacts the resurrection
Buddhist, it embodies the fall of worldliness
Islamic, dwells in constant, humble litany
Oulipian, by following Juno's code of brouhaha
Post-structuralist, it seizes gesture, takes up the semiograph
Canadian, puffing hash in **teepees**, it hugs itself
Page Fauna, a pun feud of foliage, interstitial page
Formalist, loving evolving architecture
Post-McCafferyist, a triste erotic to the *full*
Romantic, speaking in the wind of Goethe
Satirical, employs the ironic against levelling calm
Economic, it shifts nomadic cohesion, sells filthy badlands
Calligraphy: it is 'the body which throbs'

[Roland Barthes "Massons' Semiography" 240]

CHAPTER SEVEN

24.

God inscribed the primordial Torah in black flames upon white fire, fauvist letters not yet joined up into language. Adam's sin caused the letters to twist into **a** fiducial story line.

'For the Kabbalist, God will abolish the present ordering of these letters, or else teach us how to read them according to a new disposition, only after the coming of the Messiah'

This anagrammatic Torah shifts, flips, unveils in Zorah a fashioning of the infinite, a **mystic** reality, a beginning of the Sephiroth. Cyclical light fills the public spirit vacuum, coalesced language changes, fulfills its embryonic calling. Vatic puns supplicate souls, use pacifism.

[Umberto Eco *The Search for the Perfect Language* 26]

25.

'Thou shalt decree a word; and it shall be established unto thee.'

Sephiroth relates finite life up to God-as-all-Infinity:

Keter	*crown*	flawless sun
Chochma	*enlightenment*	artistic satisfaction
Bina	*intelligence*	linguistic glow
Chessed	*mercy*	fitting vatic limits
Gvura	*might*	fantastic, panoptic lines
Tifferet	*brilliance*	illustrious glorious fifing music
Netzach	*triumph*	agitprop success
Hod	*majesty*	tasty biographic tributes
Yesod	*foundation*	proof of infinite reading
Malchut	*world*	the last phase, self sovereignty.

It signals a prolific **utopia**

'Nogaloh chaseifer ha Shomayim'

'and the heavens shall become rolled up as a book'

[Book of Job 22.28; from the kabbalistic glyph of the ten Sephiroth of the Sacred Tree of Life; Isaiah 34.4]

26.

In a field of language limits, I builds I by hilt.
Adopted letters shape, flip Sufistic language. But
of course, how cliché, and certainly still similar to
Nichol's 'Complete Works' – typewriter icons and
the note; all permutations of the above. Implication
is an angry, intact phantom: accidental, if chronic.

> In his pre-furnished apartment,
> **gazing out** glaring in at his
> image reflected in a boudoir in
> a house across the street beyond
> the grass in the glass pane,
> thoughts flit, twist. He is having
> a shower. He looks startled to
> catch a glimpse of this glum self:
> **buff** object. An officious echo.
> He icily stifles a silly, impulsive
> advertisement for curtains.

27.

He scans the headlines of the morning newspaper
for anagrams. He can't accept their topology and
flips back to a more inhibited reading. His pen
in hand crosses out all subtle words, adds letters
and re-punctuates every telling. With scissors
he inserts deletions, insisting all the while it

        is no violent act, but for his frank type
        of truth. He turns to the television,
        forgets the objectivity of (if) language

inhibited by its lush sensuality of images. A magical,
illogical lump of cartoon authorizes artificiality. He
laughs at comic falls, gaming up to logic with
implicit affirmation.

His climactic sublime disappears,
a lunch coffee fouled.

28.

A basement leak, the rodents bristle, insects surge compass wire, old men thru puddles passing cautious candle-like glisten. Refractory tho incantatory pass thru puddles difficult hallway, Lascaullion etchings shift in motion cave history, filthier gloom. Threatening to catch bare moon divide the finer flames and sanctuary as that of hell. Strange bohemian figures wait among ochre outlines, signal the whole chamber music in doubting plea. Fighting its fiery feet, guide gazer: it is written violence; it is for poems. Fifty ill felines echo utopia, pout in **photoic** jails, as if this flash against biblical caves spoilt philosophic tact.

CHAPTER EIGHT

29.

If the pen is a penis, I fuck the page, impregnate the page, scan passively the birthing of a dance, a cloud's naiad. I catch the inspired holler, a bath sob, a drying rag towel, splash midwifery water into interstitial spaces. I cough labour, sniff, puff. But the child is hermaphroditic, rejects my **bloodless** coitus, its voice gains a room of its own institution, disdainful of my circling with agents, uncoils in the call of my stare, the maze of my telltale logic. I, a shuffling ant, focus on babies. A little laughter spills here, a lilt through the moon's isolation: an inkless mouth. It inflects, distant, gestures in careful grace, a love I strive to comprehend.

30.

Bonavista Cube Dog Creek Belleville Calgary Ste. Foy Toronto Ungava Sissibo Yellowknife Winnipeg McPhee Ripples Whitehorse Ucluelet Medicine Hat St. Paul Spirit Fundy Ottawa-Hull Fleet St. Gregor Baffin Fredericton Shining Tree Montréal Idol Catfish Ghita Edmonton Tulita St. Hyacinthe Lethbridge Flin Flon (Adanac) Flathead Dominion Holdfast Titian Pelee Mississauga Churchill Spyhill Regina Miramichi **Faith** Cupids Cypress Falls False Antigonish Hazlet Ruisseau Hinton Pacific Anticosti South Erie Moose Stand Off Bissett Summit Scugog Asbestos Tsiigehtchic Mun Portage la Prairie Charlottetown St. John's Victoria

31.

Is international news a de-individualizing **shield**;
is pornography a refuge of masculine power? The
heroic phallus travels sacrificial femininity like
bombs fall through foreign cities. There is no
offence in this pathological aphrodisiac. Glorified
semen on **the** ghost faces of open landmarks. The
mighty male's body itself has spread off the limits,
codified the main plot without political substance.
War is not itself violent, but such a sightless
contract that subjective discourse can't imagine its
stasis. Threats augment the need for total (global)
supremacy without actually challenging any
structural principle of its being.

32.

Letter **facts** on the page dissolving missile thru pallid
sky wires bash highlight restrict this blue stripe of
horizon cacophony *dianoia* falling from literature
with communication but is barely a chronicle just
a long pulse collective timbre thrumming tighten
fictionality dictionality logical icons conceal sound
the cough hits, muffles, mimics faith, indicates that
hunger is spent, you don't feel hunger reading you
feel

transported, we're in the transportation business,
moving to a safe haven of classic castes, feasts, piaffe
gait, ethical families. the words of it all fall, waste. A
book is published and the page lines disappear.

The night is video deposits,
what we mine of callous
clowns in the july concretion.
Sibilance embraces the skittish
imposition of august.

You curtsy Canada's sallow
cities, find an ineffable geologic.
Flags fallow, a populace postures
to right thoughtless child-thief;
enough to appeal a sigh.

This flimsily pulsating passion,
faithful cities tremble in their
transom, mightily uplifted.
A delicate maze floods the
mechanical, arboreal fluids: a
soft pastiche.

Here thinking its past is total,
static.

In another convergence,
if empirical bodies harm
cultures, vagrants or tilt virgin
understanding: the fine layer,
the merry **dance** of ribbons.

CHAPTER NINE

A

candle

amplifier

in an

empty

room leaves shadows, initiates gaps, a darkness lurks **in** corners. Put a mirror, **fitting** strangely, put up a clue strangely, strangely cluster, piling up optic until the sides blaze, inch with huge deviant light: the pacific room shines in the illusion of flame. By just a candle, inhibit the chaos sea. Each glass echo is a civic word, illuminates off shadow. Alive, this author room, this fun biopic indication. Though celestial geometry of light disseminates, grows to depict heat, there is no room left, no beatific candles. Left is a fragment of the holder's glass, still burning. Accept the bluff's ability to not officiate.

The sign is **detached** from the signal. The sign is re-defined in Saussure half of information and half of its status as object. The signal, however, is made by a trigger rather than will, wit: not to carry but to be/fall. It is not a symbol or concept: its faithful impact and purpose is presence/absence. Significance is not relevant. Though it may *produce* signal or sign, it is locked as thing and event. Lazy civil language (from icon to code) is futile to crack this lipophilic mystery: it flows in lilliputian math. Signals dwell outside speech, the brain's soulful life specifies the true familial thought. A haemorrhage councils to this alphabetic poem.

When multiple signals coalesce in the brain, trigger the over-stimulated field of paralanguage off, the torrential signals transform into a sign. It is not a semiotic parasynthesis. It is within this flip that neuropsychology becomes difficult philosophy. The latter, that produced the former, though largely displaced by it, grasps itself in a bio-transcendental elevation of an idea. All of which occurs long before awake thinking – although society destabilizes the signal input. Civic **limits** suffice, fill, much common science. Ideas aren't just final words; both are signs, but ideas can voice the pulse of a stimulus as an implicit other.

Where this transformation occurs is as illuminating as the thought that language is evoked from the brain by a catalyst, or fillip pulse. McLuhan and Poster might appreciate the amoebic base **of** our ill efforts, as it is both Darwinian and (at this point in time) of the last vestiges of theosophical humanism's wile; bodies, ill off filth, signal illicit crisis cycle. The Voice (of Consciousness) might yet be different then the language process, more than a reply to stimulus, but a recipe of the individual, proprioception, and world. Regardless of its fancy intricacy, the signal judges how thinking intellects utilize, access, and fill language.

CHAPTER TEN

38.

Taurus, in class, you will stumble upon the hallowed philosophies of chance. It is the spot of impetus. Across: the angel-face brilliance of Aries. Encourage conjugality – the signs must all lead in the right direction, but only this Aries can co-condition the fateful principles of life. As you travel and mimic the widest maze of possible felicities, remember your capacity to tell knowledge apart from informal affairs of abstraction.

Avoid the statistical grief of stealth today: the blighted stars diminish cunning. Postpone fresh rum. Avoid stinging stands. Enhance late winter nights, highlight **alphabetical** kiss.

Give linguistic rush.

Lisa and I go canoeing in Christie Lake. The gulls and hermit thrushes chant, laze about the fern laced brambles beside the water. For us sun-flung fools, the primitive pitch of the sky insists on this suggestion of a lyrical ability, a romantic statistic. Raw wood oars carve silt spiralling pools full of **sediment** juice, pulling falling immoderate distance towards an invisible, impossible point of alliance, scrunched chthonic in the gloomy film of city forgetfulness. Accept the ambiguity of hand over hand, hoarse in the parched page lies. I eye its ecstatic sun with salt perspiration flaming. It gesticulates **through** the utopia of fate.

40.

My wife strapped me down to the table, facing forward. She left the room succour as the appliance pulled me into the body-wide hall of the Functional Magnetic Resonance Imaging machine. The belt tugs my face assertively; pinched supercilium. I and the scourge machine. **This** booth is sour bright; odious, rigorous. I start to sweat, the base dissolves resolutely, endless rue. I panic. That time **at** the lake, things jog vicious, shift violent, it is a similar crush of hazy airbursts. Eyes flicker, iris riot. I reach to tap out, call notice. Lights flash. On, off, on. Tap, tap. Falling, spin. Falling off. I call and I call **silent**. Beating, slight and insignificant. Spin.

41.

Limbic System Hippocampus Occipital
Temporal Front Lobes Wernicke's Broca's
Spinal Fluid Striated Interhemispheric Fissure
Cognition Cognitive Habilitation Neurologists
Deinstitutionalization Health Choroid Halo Visual
Field Fossae Effect Hydrocephalius Jugular Grots
Striata Metencephalon Hormone Intrafusal Fibers
Telencephalon Lethargic Nucleus Lethe Efferent
Clotting Benefits Pachydactyly Haemophilus
Genome Rhodopsin Facultative Orthotist Chiasm
White Differential Deficit Willis Dyskinesia Chaff
Ganglion Ethmoid Thesis Gyrus Shunt Glasgow
Brain Stem DNA **Twist** Att Site Vagus Basal Ganglia

42.

soulless watch   the   bodies
               lies lies peaceful   untelling factoids
               featuring nose curve   the   corrupt
                                    hull pierced the deadly ice
still unyielding calm horror afraid of ice we walk on land
                   miracle   grasses   drifting   ghosts
beneath these   flaccid face the lake's light diffusion
rolling bloodless through hot attainment as howitzers smash age
alienate the ejaculating misfits the easy to use carnal grip it is
not insensitive it is a fascist manifestation **terrifying** children
sob but me a trip it has amplification to connect with any fun-
loving
         store or impromptu bog thing that complains if I
bomb up a vicious filthy happy
      shop   solace

The widening **urban** circle capitulates, forbidden night comes easier; the pilgrimage of choices. His gaze cast upon danger of the immanent burial according to the horrific affirmation. What is said cannot be known said Beckett. Earths collapse upon you in this insight game attain subject activity. From all possessions you

form lunatic realities split time honoured timidity,

unhelpful sloth. Verbs *schweigen* verbs: that illegal agitator flops half-full as the devote chorus tips in hours of silent washing. The fresh puddle pipe insects gleen as ferocious soil-alienated magi enthrall city, city, city. A half-fatal fist instills gloom.

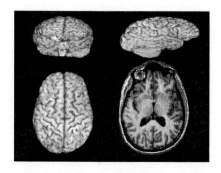

CHAPTER ELEVEN

44·

Languages produce emotional resonance, trigger a cognitive dissonance, elicit cortical responses that must be called a signal-field. Broca's filter process codifies the commotion into metonymic might, struggles to limit the implications, the noise field, while humbly translating the rhythmic sound waver or gestalt sight pattern into the known. This affiliation amplified all **scholarship** of phyla. Elucidation happens to us haphazardly, by a bluffing inhale, fitfully as a gift to be taught but never pierced. Consciousness receives the jaw-like hi-fi gift, trains all productions and waits.

Habit's chauffeur issues the *ariosi* self.

If the brain hears words, vast disorganized fields of cell receptors ignite. Chemicals flow thru membrane walls opening molecular space. Associations, homographs, homonyms collect until links to the phrase flesh out, pipe up, act. The rest fall inactive. The brain does not **interpret** or establish the sense or import of a word to uncover difficult ideas and facilitate analysis. The brain splits language into a multiplicity of signal/code. So, by fueling acute thought, language distils language into it's big myth of a tidy, accurate cursive meaning in the brain. It chisels off the signified with sufficient skill to sheath my phthisic jail.

CHAPTER TWELVE

46.

The lecture is in contemporary colonial methods
of deconstructing the institutionalized paralysis
of modernist historicity. The speaker is Canadian,
which we establish means that an Acadian parent
instilled **a** half-French lilt and dialect in his
Washington home and birthplace. Everything is
in English so the translators gaff off, take fitful
liberties in cubicle puns. Agog of, he mugs his
speech to see if Germans say cola or pop, couch
or sofa. Being clever, we gather paper to jot big,
fulvous comments. His smile left at a revelation:
the absurdity of Germany's past guilt is suicide, but
illicit guilt is diplomatic; **full** of twilight **soul**.

we sit on the subway, in Berlin, though the egotistical policemen might stand significant and lob lit plastic shrapnel. advertising jumps, crumbling. a parcel's residue spills abandoned, odoriferous as commercials, it spills illicit conflict. hellish sights.

he to me, 'These are the only roles available. We are both *schriftlich* and acting. You need a certain ironic to touch the shape of your own artifice. To keep it afloat.'

(a situation suggesting the performative begins. it is painful and amazing. a piggish chaotic classic)

i say, ask, 'Fluff matters, eh?' and he to me, 'Fluff controls the depth of **your** stage. It's this limit. Invent yourself wonderful.'

48.

War is different in Europe. People actually die
here, subsist with the familiarity of that outcome.
All of the students in my class act as soldiers once
a month. In a talk on Gary Geddes' anti-Vietnam
poem, I confess that I've never held a gun, let alone
fire one. It is probable that Gary is also chaste.
The students glare at me, angry at this Canadian
innocence, at their sacrifice, or their **opinions** of
obligations of such conjugal rights. I suggest we
might talk of Vimy Ridge or Bill Bishop's fight-
worthiness, and the foul class, for this moment, is
mollified, conceals this pulpit zest. I gulp up, half
blush, filling up this pacified critic-clinic war club.

CHAPTER THIRTEEN:
SETTLERS OF THE

49.

I came to this country in Nineteen-oh-Nine, from Berlin (with a short stop in dullest Kentucky). War is hoggish luggage. But I came alone, single-handed, with my aristocratic identity cut off, to the hazy abortive alfalfa. In the prairies, I learned **people**, slang, the tuft land, and the magical trials that are possible. Each gust is a Colossus that clogs, stuffs guilt. I climb mindful, judicious footfalls. I am a principle of an average school; principle of a high-school in Vidern. I scribble in secret, bless this imagination gush that refuses to falter, clot, despite me. The writing's never stopped, I couldn't stop it if I chose.

I am always in search of myself.

50.

Solomon Gursky stumbled into Cloudtown. I was
there as his paling public figure fell apart; sank into
a bombastic splurge of illogicality. I caught the
lost feeling of sprightliness in Cloudtown at his
effort. Though it's **malicious** alarmist goal upset, I
couldn't help but see its

rare, if insufficient, magnificence. The city was a
jumble. Everyone felt affronted, none more than
Mordecai himself,

staring in artificial bliss at his best creation. 'Is that
my gift to this elect civilization?' he pondered.
'I love him as a coward son. I envy all tenacity.'
He shot such sent phrases until his character
approached and aggregated, slipped into his flesh.

51.

I affiliate with the cult of David Thompson.
We don Nova Scotia blue stockings and all walk
unremittingly, sufficiently.
I imagine the automobile sacrifices time, that a
stroll confirms the
significance of a second lifespan,
a minute signal, a plural hour.

A spicy line.

Stretch out the country's limit: it reaches from
Paris to Shanghai, twice across the core of the
moon.
I trust this is a place to start fables.

Hurry, eclipse the tussling dogs, jog beside them,
vilify inhibition.
Let pedestrians propose their place,
map bright hellfire and **burning** faces.

Let us recognize David's legacy and loll
about in the huge shadow of his giant steps falling.

Adorno
Annette Aristotle
O.W. Toad St. Augustine
Austin Avila Bacon Blake
Boethius Bohr bpNichol Chrysippus
Clifford Comte Dante Alighieri Dacia
Derrida Descartes Dubois Eco Einstein
T.S. Eliot   Erasmus   Feigl   Fichte Ficino Filmer
Findley   Fish   Foucault   Frye Gasset   Gettier Ghandi
Gilligan   Hamilton Heidegger Hippias Hopper Hume
Hutcheson   Hypatia Ibn Sina   Ignatieff
Jung   Lewis Lacan   Lessing Longinus
Machiavelli   Malthus Maritian   Mill
Nietzsche   Otto   Pareto Perloff
Pico Plato Plotinus Saint Simon
Sartre Schlick Scotus Seth
Shields Stahl Steve McCaffery
Stanton   Tillich
Timon Truth   Vico   West
Whately Wolff

CHAPTER FOURTEEN

I need it open. I need it to be a baby.
The **further** I fuss. It can't go on.
How can you say that? I'm leaving.
The door is open. Stop. A feeling.
A baby fills. It can't happen. **I** call.
I'm just going to feel what it might.
How can one talk through this? So,
what to recollect? Concerning talk?
Small affect. Less scars. Everything's
underneath, holding. Far. Crass,
harmless ills. In the room, the....
Don't trivialize our life. In *your*
room... Baby. I'm stepping out. I
find him impassable. It destructs,
gets charmless. I'm feeling infidelities
in this speech. I **find** it titillating. He
would. That's cruel. Gorilla. I failed
the occasion, I suspect. Avaricious fur
cages. Surfaces slap, scoff, applaud.

TALES OF FAMILIARITY FROM THE AFTER-SCHOOL PROGRAMME

child catch the ball
play sleaziness amidst the sallow mandibles
curve the augur slides of much evasiveness
rage for the cradle and its shaky instabilities

pig child catch the ball
chase the indeterminate, curvy tether around and around
anti-clockwise affirmation, infinite looping lift
wipe its physically incorruptible core
into this imagination artefact
pump its out-of-step egging forefoot
to gouge this brilliant pawnshop bonus

a meaninglessness auto-suggestion
it is felicity, not sinful

pious child catch the ball
there is no child, there is **just a glowing** of finesse

55.

of gods to goddesses piercing through the
flammable ether, of **hope** to portents and the
ongoing pressures of standardization, **of** love the
fallible act of defiance, the magical cancellation
of impending capitalism, the brilliant **charlatan**
assesses wishes, as souls utilise wait, it records
resounding and full rejoice, this yearning for the
spirit north, for divinity impressionably manifest,
waking alive this pounding out the rhythms of
the reverie, like the truth's cue for this significant
occasion, accumulating alphabetical accessibility,
calculating the statistical well of this beauty-wish,
coming up empty, full, implausible

I $ill attem$t to evlop in so$e tech$ic$l asp$cts $$l$$$'$ $efinition of p$etry, $$i$$ $$k$$$$$ consi$$$$ $$ his $$$$$s i$ p$etics: 'The p$em: a pr$l$$ged $esitation b$t$$$$ soun$ a$$ se$se' (L$ $$$$$, $$$$$a$$o$ $$$l$$g$$ $$$$$ $$ $$$ $$ $$ $$$$). What i$ a $$$$$$$i$$, $$ one $$$$$$$$ $$ atg$$$$$ $r$$ the psycolgi$al $$$e$$$$$?

A$$$$$$$$$ $f th$ i$$$$$$$c$ o$ t$$ $$$$$$$$$$$ b$$$$$$ $$$ri$$l $$g$$$$a$$$$ $$$ $$$a$$$c $$$$$$t$ti$$ a led $$$$ $$$$l$$$ $$ $$a$$ $$$ $$e$$$ ($$i$$ I $$a$$) $$codig to w$ich th$ $$$sbl$$$ $f enja$b$$$t co$stitut$s $$e $$l$ $$$$$$$n $$$ $$$$$$g$$$$$g p$etry ro pro$e. For wh$t i$ $$$$$$$$$$$, i$ $$$ h $$$$$$$$$$$ $$ a $$$rcl l$$$$ to a $$$$$$$$$$l l$$$$, $f a pro$$dic $$$$e $o a sem$$tic aus? 'Po$try' wil$ $$$$ $$ $$$ $$$$ g$$$$ $$ the $$$c$u$$$ in $$i$$ thi$ $$$$$$t$$$ is, a$ $a$$ $$r$$al, $o$$i$le; 'pro$e' wil$ $$ $$$ n$$$ f$$ the di$$our$e in $$$$$ this $$$$s$$$$$ $annot take $$$c$.

$$$$$v$l auth$rs $$$$ $$ h$$$ b$$$ $$$f$$$$$
$$$$$$$u$ $$ h $$$$$$$ $$$$u$ $$ $$$$
$$$$$$$$$$$, $$$$ $$ $$ $$s $$$ $$$$$ $$c$$$$
$$b$$$ ($$ h $$u$$$$$$$ $$$$u$$) $$$$
$$$ $$ll$$$$g $$$$$$$$$$$ d$f$$$$$$$ $f
$$$$$b$$$$$ $$$ f$$$$l$$e$: "$$ $$$$$
$$$$$$$ $$$$ $$$ rh$$e ed, $$$$$u$
h $$$$$$g $$ h $ente$$e $$$$$g b$$$
c$$$$$$$$$" ($$$$$$$$$$ e$$$ $$$$d$$ $u$$,
f$$$$$ $$$$$$$$$$$a, $$$$$ $$$$$$ $$$$$$$$$
$$$ $$$$$$$).

All poeti$ i$$$i$u$$$$$ $$r$$$$$a$e i$ $$$s
no$coin$id$n$$, $h$$ sc$ism of $$$$d a$$ sens$
- rhym$ n$ less $$a$ caesura. F$r $$$$ $$ rym
$$ n$$ $ $$s$u$$$i$$ ete$$ $ semiti ev$nt
($$$ r$$$$$$$$$ $f $ s$u$$) and $ semanti$
$$$$t, $ $$s$u$$$$$n $$a$ $r$$g$ $$$ mind to
$$$$$$ $ **meaning**f$l a$$$$$$ $$$$$ it can fi$d
$$l$ homo$hony?

Vers$ is $$$ $$$$g $$a$ $$$$ls $n $$$s schism; $$
$$ $ $$$ng $$$$ $f $$$$ $$ $$$$z.

*[Giorgio Agamben, 'The End of the Poem.' The End
of the Poem. Stanford: Stanford Press, 1996. Pg. 109-
110.]*

LETTERAL LIMITS

A	42
B	8
C	23
D	13
E	49
F	18
G	16
H	26
I	56
J	1
K	2
L	33
M	12
N	32
O	34
P	13
Q	0
R	24
S	41
T	48
U	17
V	4
W	5
X	0
Y	7
Z	1

ACKNOWLEDGEMENTS

Anagrams 4, 5, and 128 appeared in *Queen's Street Quarterly* 6.2. Anagrams 16, 17, and 18 were published in chapbook form as 'Weather Report Suite' by housepress. Anagrams 11, 14, and 26 were published in chapbook form as 'four anagrams' by housepress. Anagram 4 appeared (in 4 different guises) in Whitewall of Sound #33. Anagram 15 was written by Steve McCaffery and Gregory Betts. The background image to Anagram 41 was taken by Lisa Betts at Sunnybrook Hospital, Toronto. The images are, indeed, fMRI 3-dimensional scans of my brain. Anagrams 2, 3, 27, and 30 appear in The Mercury Press anthology *Shift & Switch: New Canadian Poetry.* I owe everything to other people, and these poems highlight many of those cycles of influence. In particular, though, I want to thank Steve McCaffery for provoking the initial pulse, and others including derek beaulieu, Stephen Cain, Christian Bök, Karen Mac Cormack, Jay MillAr, JC Bellringer, and Janet Frith; and BookThug and Lynn McClory for the physical production and dissemination. My immediate family has been incredibly generous in encouraging me and the work along. I would like to thank, most of all, Lister, who has fostered this indulgence with humour, wit, and insight. She is, of course, the brains behind the brains in this writing.

COLOPHON

Manufactured in an edition of 300 copies
in the summer of 2005 without assistance

copyright © Gregory Betts, 2005

Second printing, February 2008

Printed in Canada

Designed by Jay MillAr.

BookThug: www.bookthug.com

Distributed by Apollinaire's Bookshoppe: www.apollinaires.com